Fact Finders®

Amazing Animal Colonies

BEES AND WASPS

Secrets of Their Busy Colonies

by Sara L. Latta

raintree
a Capstone company — publishers for children

Raintree is an imprint of Capstone Global Library Limited, a company incorporated in England and Wales having its registered office at 264 Banbury Road, Oxford, OX2 7DY – Registered company number: 6695582

www.raintree.co.uk
myorders@raintree.co.uk

Edited by Carrie Braulick Sheely
Designed by Ted Williams
Original illustrations © Capstone Global Library Limited 2019
Picture research by Heather Mauldin
Production by Katy LaVigne
Originated by Capstone Global Library Ltd
Printed and bound in India

ISBN 978 1 4747 7094 1
23 22 21 20 19
10 9 8 7 6 5 4 3 2 1

British Library Cataloguing in Publication Data
A full catalogue record for this book is available from the British Library.

Acknowledgements
We would like to thank the following for permission to reproduce photographs: Alamy: Deborah Lee Rossiter, 16, frans lemmens, 24; Getty Images: Paul Starosta, 23; iStockphoto: Ale-ks, 7 (top), bigemrg, 8 (middle), borchee, 27 (inset), macroworld, 7 (bottom), witoldkr1, 18; Minden Pictures: Francois Gilson, 11; Shutterstock: Alexey Laputin, 21, BlueRingMedia, 15, Daniel Prudek, cover (top right), 4, 8 (top), Elliotte Rusty Harold, 25, Grezova Olga, 9 (bottom), Irina Kozorog, 27, Ivan Godal, 9 (top), l i g h t p o e t, cover (bottom), 1, Leonid Eremeychuk, cover (background), macondo, 28, Marco Uliana, 9 (middle), Poppap pongsakorn, cover (top left), SaraJo, 19, Shishka4, 14, stefanolunardi, 13, Suwat Sirivutcharungchit, 6, YapAhock, 8 (bottom).

Every effort has been made to contact copyright holders of material reproduced in this book. Any omissions will be rectified in subsequent printings if notice is given to the publisher.

All the internet addresses (URLs) given in this book were valid at the time of going to press. However, due to the dynamic nature of the internet, some addresses may have changed, or sites may have changed or ceased to exist since publication. While the author and publisher regret any inconvenience this may cause readers, no responsibility for any such changes can be accepted by either the author or the publisher.

Contents

CHAPTER ONE
THE BUZZ ON BEES AND WASPS

A honey bee collects nectar from a flower.

4

A honey bee flies around on a sunny day. It lands on a flower. It collects **nectar** from the flower. The bee carries the nectar back to its nest. It passes the nectar to other bees. These bees break down the nectar. It turns into honey. They put the honey into cells in the nest. The young bees in the **colony** will eat the honey. Thousands of honey bees repeat these jobs throughout the day. It's all in a day's work to keep the colony growing.

On the social side

There are thousands of **species** of bees and wasps. They all belong to the **insect** group Hymenoptera. Some of these bees and wasps live in highly social colonies.

Bumble bees and honey bees are two of the most common types of social bees. Honey bees live throughout the world except in very cold places near the polar regions. Bumble bees mainly live in Europe, North America and Asia. Some also live in South America.

nectar sweet liquid found in many flowers

colony large group of insects that live together

species group of closely related organisms that can produce offspring

insect small animal with a hard outer shell, six legs, three body sections and two antennae

Stingless bees are another type of social bee. They live in Africa, Australia and South America. Although they cannot sting, they do defend themselves with painful bites.

Hornets, yellow jackets and paper wasps are common types of social wasps. Most hornets live in warm parts of Asia. They also live in Europe, Africa and North America. Yellow jackets and paper wasps live in most areas of the world except in the polar regions.

Stingless bees mainly live in warm tropical regions.

BEES VS WASPS

Bees and wasps are closely related. Many people get them confused. But it's easy to tell them apart once you know what to look for. Bees have a round **abdomen** and **thorax**. They have flat, wide legs that are generally not seen while flying. They are covered with fuzzy hairs.

bee

wasp

Wasps have a slender abdomen and thorax. They also have slender legs shaped like cylinders. Their legs hang below the body during flight. Their bodies are usually smooth and shiny.

abdomen back section of an insect's body

thorax middle section of an insect's body; wings and legs are attached to the thorax

One for all

Social bees and wasps live and work in highly organized colonies. Each colony is like a large, close family. Each individual member is an organism. It can act alone. But it can't survive without the rest. The organisms depend on each other. Each member works to help the whole colony. Scientists call the colonies of these social insects **super-organisms**.

COMMON SOCIAL BEES

honey bee
number of species worldwide: 7

bumble bee
number of species worldwide:
about 250

stingless bee
number of species worldwide:
400–500

COMMON SOCIAL WASPS

hornet
number of species worldwide: 25

yellow jacket
number of species worldwide:
about 40

paper wasp
number of species worldwide:
about 500

super-organism group of living things that
work together as one whole

CHAPTER TWO
LIFE IN A COLONY

Members of a social bee or wasp colony work together in one nest. Nests are busy places. Some colonies have thousands of members. A honey bee colony can have as many as 80,000 members!

Each colony member has an important job. The colony members are divided into three different **castes**: queen, drone and worker.

Castes in social bee colonies

Social bee colonies have just one queen at a time. The queen bee lays all the eggs in the colony. She lays both **fertilized** and unfertilized eggs. Fertilized eggs develop into workers or queens. Unfertilized eggs develop into drones.

caste group within a colony that does a certain job
fertilize join an egg of a female with a sperm of a male to produce young

10

Worker bees make a substance called royal jelly. They feed it to all of the young for the first three days of life. They also continue feeding it to any young that will become queens. Workers feed royal jelly to the adult queen in the colony throughout her life.

A worker bee feeds a developing queen inside a royal cell.

Worker bees are all female. They do not lay eggs, but they have many important jobs. Workers gather a powdery substance made by plants, called pollen. They also gather nectar from flowers. They use the nectar to make honey to feed the young bees in the nest. They also feed pollen to the young. Workers protect the colony from enemies. They are also nest builders and cleaners.

Drones have only one job. They mate with the queen. Queens and drones mate outside the nest in mid-air. The drones die shortly after mating.

Castes in social wasp colonies

Social wasp castes are similar to those of social bees. Most wasp species have only one queen in each colony. The drone's only job is to mate with the queen. The workers care for the young in the nest. Many species hunt for insects and spiders to bring back to the young. Adult wasps feed mainly on nectar or sweet fruit.

Worker bees feed developing bees inside cells.

From egg to adult

As bees and wasps become adults, they go through different stages. The queen bee or wasp lays an egg. The egg hatches into a larva. A larva sheds its skin (moults) as it grows. The larva wraps itself in a case called a cocoon. At this stage, the developing bee or wasp is called a pupa. When the bee or wasp comes out of the cocoon it is an adult.

⬆ wasp larvae and pupae

LIFE CYCLE OF A HONEY BEE

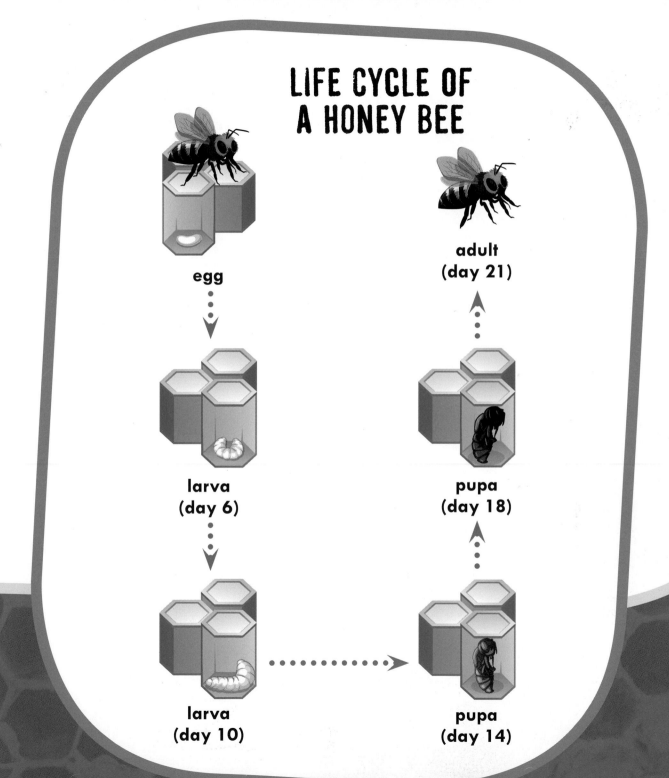

egg

larva
(day 6)

larva
(day 10)

pupa
(day 14)

pupa
(day 18)

adult
(day 21)

CHAPTER THREE

HOME SWEET HOME

↑ Honey bees often make their nests inside hollow trees.

Bees and wasps are master builders. Their nests need to be dry and safe from enemies. They must support the weight of the colony. Bee nests may need to support the weight of a lot of honey.

Honey bee nests

Honey bees often build their nests in hollow trees or small caves. The nests are made of wax **hexagon**-shaped cells. These connected hexagons make the nest very strong.

The wax cells are arranged in layers. These sheets are called honeycombs. The bees use their mouthparts to place the wax on the growing comb. Honey bees build storage cells for honey and pollen on the edges and at the top of the comb. They build cells for the developing bees in the centre and lower part of the comb. There are no special cells for adult bees. They move about on the surface of the comb.

hexagon shape with six straight sides

Bumble bee nests

Some bumble bee species build their nests in abandoned rodent holes in the ground. Others make nests in thick grass, in trees or under the eaves of buildings.

Like honey bees, bumble bees also use wax cells to make their nests. But the cells of a bumble bee's nest are clustered together untidily. Bumble bees often line their nests with material such as leaves or animal fur. These materials help to keep the nests warm.

Bumble bee nests are often in holes in the ground.

Wasp nests

Social wasps choose different places for their nests depending on the species. Paper wasps build umbrella-shaped nests underneath the eaves of buildings or the outcroppings of rocks. Hornets build rugby-ball-shaped nests in high places such as treetops or hollow tree trunks. Yellow jackets often build underground nests. They may use abandoned rodent dens or make nests in hollow tree stumps.

Social wasps build their nests out of paper. They make this paper themselves. They use their jaws to scrape bits of wood from trees or even cardboard. They mix the wood fibres with saliva to make a **pulp**.

pulp mixture of ground-up paper and saliva

CHAPTER FOUR

COMMUNICATING WITHOUT WORDS

When you're working on a team project, you probably talk a lot to your team members. Good communication helps get the work done. Social bees and wasps cannot speak. But they communicate in other ways.

Using pheromones

Social bees and wasps communicate mainly with chemicals called **pheromones**. Queen bees and wasps release a chemical that tells the colony, "I'm still here!" The chemical keeps most larvae from becoming queens. Other queen chemicals attract drones when it is time to mate. Hungry larvae give off chemicals that signal workers to feed them. Workers release chemicals that say, "Follow me!" These chemicals can help other workers to find their way back to the nest or to a food source.

20

Birds, bears, reptiles and other animals eat bees and wasps. Social bees and wasps release alarm chemicals when they sting an attacker near the nest. The chemicals send signals to the rest of the colony members that they should attack. If these defenders die, even more alarm pheromones are released.

pheromone chemical released by animals that causes other members of the species to behave in a certain way

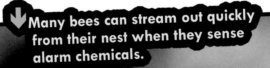

Many bees can stream out quickly from their nest when they sense alarm chemicals.

Dancing honey bees

Honey bees also dance to communicate. A worker bee that has found nectar leaves her own scent on the flowers. She returns to the hive and feeds other bees. Then she begins to dance. If the food is near the hive, she will dance in a circle, switching directions occasionally. The other worker bees can smell the scent of the flowers on the dancing bee. They use it to help them locate the food source. The scent the first bee left on the flowers also guides the other workers.

Sometimes a bee finds a food source far away from the hive. The bee may then do the "**waggle** dance". She waggles her tail several times while travelling in a straight line. Then she turns right and returns to the starting point. She does another waggle and turns left, again returning to her starting point. The dance tells other bees the direction and distance to the flowers.

AMAZING FACT

Honey bees may fly up to 4.8 kilometres (3 miles) to find nectar. Bumble bees stay closer to home. They travel up to about 1.6 kilometres (1 mile).

waggle move from side to side

↑ A worker bee does a waggle dance to alert other bees to a food source.

Listen up!

Some bees and wasps use sound or vibration to communicate. For years, scientists have noticed that some wasps drum their abdomens against different parts of the nest in a certain rhythm. They thought it was a sign of hunger. In 2018, scientists studied this behaviour in German yellow jackets. They saw that the behaviour decreased when food sources were low. The scientists think wasps may use the drumming to get other wasps to come to a food source.

Queens sometimes make a piping noise. Scientists believe queens pipe for different reasons. An old queen may pipe when a nest has got too big. The piping may be a signal to workers that it's time to leave. A new queen that has come out of her cell often pipes. She may be signalling to queens still in their cells that she is willing to fight. Sometimes the new queen kills the developing queen bees.

A queen (centre) may have many different ways of communicating with the colony's workers.

NEVER FORGET A FACE

To people, wasp faces probably look alike. But not to members of the paper wasp species *Polistes fuscatus*. These paper wasps have more than one queen in each nest. Some queens have a higher rank than others. Scientists think this is why the wasps have the ability to recognize different faces. It may help the wasps to avoid conflict. Wasp species with only one queen in each colony can't tell each other apart.

Members of the *Polistes fuscatus* wasp species are golden brown.

CHAPTER FIVE

BEES, WASPS AND PEOPLE

Bees and wasps are all around us. We come into contact with them often. While bees and wasps can cause painful stings, they also help people in many ways.

Ouch!

Wasps and most bees can sting. Only the females sting. Wasps and bees are most likely to sting if they think you are threatening them or their nests. Wasps tend to be more aggressive than bees. Wasps and most bees can sting over and over again. Other bees, such as honey bees, can sting only once before they die.

When they sting, wasps and bees inject a poisonous liquid called venom with a stinger. The stings cause pain and swelling for a short time. People who have an **allergy** to bee and wasp venom need to get medical help straight away if they are stung. If not, they may die.

allergy extremely high sensitivity to something in the environment

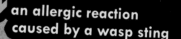
an allergic reaction
caused by a wasp sting

HOW TO AVOID
BEING STUNG

A bee or wasp buzzing around you can be scary. But you can take action to avoid being stung. Stay patient and calm. Let the insect leave on its own. Swatting at it or flapping your arms will make it more likely to sting. If you do get stung, wash the area with soap and water to remove the venom. Apply an ice pack to reduce swelling and pain.

Bees, wasps and crops

Bees and wasps help plants to grow. As bees travel from one flower to another, they transfer pollen from plant to plant on their hairy legs. The pollen allows the plants to make new seeds. Farmers rely on bees to pollinate many crops. Nearly one-third of the food we eat comes from bee-pollinated fruit, vegetables or nuts. Wasps kill many insects that destroy crops. These pests include grubs and caterpillars.

Sweet honey

Honey bees make a great deal of honey. Beekeepers keep honey bees in hives. They take the extra honey from the hives to eat or sell.

Beekeepers wear protective suits to protect them from stings.

People have used honey to make medicine since ancient times. Some people believe honey helps treat wounds, coughs, dandruff, sore throats and allergies.

Vanishing honey bees

Honey bee populations are in decline. Scientists believe there are a variety of reasons for this decline. Pesticides used to kill insects that harm plants kill many bees. Other bees may be affected by loss of **habitat**. The flowers that bees need to collect food from are then harder for them to find. Further decline of honey bee populations may cause food shortages and harm the **ecosystem**.

Many people are working to increase honey bee numbers. They plant flowers and encourage farmers to avoid widespread use of chemicals.

The next time bees and wasps buzz around your picnic, don't swat them away. Think about all the benefits they bring to our world.

habitat natural place and conditions in which a plant or animal lives

ecosystem group of animals and plants that work together with their surroundings

Glossary

abdomen back section of an insect's body

allergy extremely high sensitivity to something in the environment

caste group within a colony that does a certain job

colony large group of insects that live together

ecosystem group of animals and plants that work together with their surroundings

fertilize join an egg of a female with a sperm of a male to produce young

habitat natural place and conditions in which a plant or animal lives

hexagon shape with six straight sides

insect small animal with a hard outer shell, six legs, three body sections and two antennae

nectar sweet liquid found in many flowers

pheromone chemical released by animals that causes other members of the species to behave in a certain way

pulp mixture of ground-up paper and saliva

species group of closely related organisms that can produce offspring

super-organism group of living things that work together as one whole

thorax middle section of an insect's body

waggle move from side to side

Find out more

Books

The Bee Book, Charlotte Milner (DK Children, 2018)

Bees and Wasps, James Maclaine (Usborne, 2013)

Insects (Pocket Eyewitness), DK (DK Children, 2018)

Websites

www.bbc.com/bitesize/articles/zx4ktv4
Learn more about why bees are attracted to flowers.

www.dkfindout.com/uk/animals-and-nature/insects/bee-colonies
Find out more about bee colonies.

Comprehension questions

1. Why do you think hexagon shapes keep a bee or wasp nest stronger than using other shapes would? Use other reference books or the internet to support your answer.
2. Name three similarities and three differences between bee and wasp colonies.
3. Bees are one type of insect that forms colonies. Use other reference books or the internet to research other types of insects that live in colonies. Compare these colonies with bee and wasp colonies.

Index